# Canadian Heritage Bread Making
### by
### Debra Rebryna

LONE
PINE

**Homeworld**

*The Publisher:*
**Lone Pine Publishing**
#206, 10426-81 Avenue
Edmonton, Alberta, Canada
T6E 1X5

**Canadian Cataloguing in Publication Data**
Rebryna, Debra
Canadian Heritage Breadmaking

(Homeworld)
Includes index.
ISBN 1-55105-016-1

1. Cookery (Bread) I.Title. II. Series.

TX769.R42 1992  641.8'15  C92-091753-4

Original Compilation: *Debra Rebryna*
Editorial: *Debby Shoctor, Lloyd Dick, Gary Whyte*
Homeworld Editor: *Lloyd Dick*
Cover Illustration: *Linda Dunn*
Original Illustrations: *Doris Chaput*
Printing: *Friesen Printers. Altona, Manitoba, Canada*

The publisher gratefully acknowledges the assistance of
the Federal Department of Communications, Alberta
Culture and Multiculturalism and financial support
provided by the Alberta Foundation for the Arts in the
production of this book

# Contents

# Bread Made Easy

Bread has been a staple of man's diet for many thousands of years. It started out as simple unleavened loaves baked over hot stones, evolving into the heavy, yeasty loaves Roman bakers sold from their stone ovens and later developing into all the variations we bake today in our modern kitchens.

Perhaps because of those long ago origins and the fact that our grandmothers and probably our mothers baked many of the breads we enjoyed while growing up, especially for holidays and special occasions, bread making has become an intrinsic part of our feelings of home and family. Rich with tradition in many of our ethnic backgrounds, it is difficult to name that feeling of immense satisfaction one gets when pulling a freshly baked, golden brown loaf from your oven and sharing it with family and friends.

This book is intended to introduce the novice bread maker to the wide world of bread through recipes that are significant to the cultures from which they come (so you too, can bake with pride the loaves that are part of your family heritage). The emphasis is on the recipes and techniques that will allow you to learn the art of bread making and help you to achieve good results every time. To add to your enjoyment, I have included some interesting historical and cultural information with each recipe.

# Ingredients

## Flour

All-purpose flour (a mixture of hard and soft wheats) is used for most recipes in this book unless otherwise specified. Other types of flours and cereals — whole wheat, rye, cornmeal and oatmeal — are usually added in combination with all-purpose to give us specialty breads and loaves. The flour does not need to be sifted — simply fill your measure full and level off the top. Wheat flour contains gluten and when the flour is mixed with liquid into a dough and kneaded the gluten stretches and forms a framework that holds the gas given off by the growing yeast. This process is what makes the dough rise. Recipes give approximate amounts of flour necessary because flour's ability to absorb moisture changes — on a humid summer day your flour may absorb more liquid so more flour is necessary to produce a smooth non-sticky dough whereas on a dry winter day less flour will be needed to produce the same result.

## Yeast

Yeast is the leavener that makes the dough rise. It is a living organism and when we add the right combination of moisture and warmth (warm water) and food (sugar) it begins to grow. As it grows it gives off carbon dioxide gas. This gas is then caught in the gluten strands made when you kneaded the dough, causing the dough to rise. Because yeast needs the right conditions to grow, carefully follow the recommended measurements and liquid temperatures when dissolving the yeast.

There are many types of yeast available on the market today. With experience, you will be able to choose which one works best for you. For simplicity, the recipes in the book all use active dry yeast. No matter what you are using, always check the "best before" date on your package before you start. If the date has passed, check the yeast action before assembling other ingredients. The yeast may not work and then your bread will not rise. Most recipes use one of the two methods above to begin yeast action.

---

### Types of Yeast

- **Traditional or water dissolve method:** dry yeast is gently stirred into lukewarm water (105 - 115° F) in which sugar has been dissolved (1 tsp. sugar to 1/2 cup water for 1 Tbsp. yeast). **Note: 1 Tbsp. yeast = 1 package**. Let stand 10 minutes, then stir well. Traditional yeasts use this method, quick or rapid rise yeasts can also be used this way with good results.
- **Quick mix method:** the dry yeast is added to 1/4 the amount of flour called for in the recipe along with the other dry ingredients. Then warm liquids (120 - 135° F) are added tot he dry ingredients and the two are beaten together. Additional flour is then added following recipe directions. Only certain types of yeast give good results with this method — read package directions carefully.

## Baking Powder and Baking Soda

These two products are also leaveners, usually used in quick breads and muffins. They react with other ingredients or conditions to produce carbon dioxide gas that makes the dough or batter rise. Baking soda reacts with acids, i.e. buttermilk or orange juice. The reaction happens very quickly so ingredients must be assembled and baked promptly. Baking powder reacts somewhat to additional ingredients but does its primary work when it is exposed to the heat of the oven during baking.

## Liquids

Water and milk are the usual liquids used in bread making. Fruit juices, water from cooking potatoes and other liquids are sometimes called for. Milk may be whole, skim, evaporated or non-fat dry. Any liquid must be warmed before using to keep up the yeast action. Breads made with milk have a softer, smoother texture and whiter crumb than breads made with water, which are crisper-crusted and have a more wheaty flavour.

## Fat

Shortening, butter, margarine and vegetable oils are all used in bread baking to give flavour and improve texture. Fat lubricates the dough, making it easier for the gluten to stretch as gas forms in rising.

## Eggs

These are used to add richness in colour and flavour to breads. They also add nutrition and food value. Breads made with eggs have a finer-textured crumb. Eggs can be beaten and brushed on the top of the loaf to give the bread a golden brown crust when baked. See **Glazes**.

## Sugar, Salt and Seasonings

Sugar is an ingredient necessary for proper yeast action. Along with salt and seasonings, it adds flavour to baked products.

## Glazes

A glaze is brushed on a baked or unbaked loaf to improve flavour and appearance. Instructions for glazing are usually given in the recipe but are always optional. They may be a part of the ingredients of the loaf (oatmeal on an oatmeal bread or a dusting of flour on rolls) or they may be used to hold decorative additions like sesame seeds or herbs to the top of the loaf.

An egg wash (beaten egg with 1 tsp. water or milk) will hold additional ingredients and will also give a shiny crust as will a brushing of milk or cream. Melted butter, margarine or oil can be brushed on either before or after baking to give a soft, shiny crust. Sweet glazes are usually brushed on after baking to make the crust shiny and add flavour. Granulated or icing sugar mixed with water is a typical glaze, but flavourings can be added or warmed honey or jelly can be used for a different and individual touch.

# *Utensils*

- Standard liquid and dry measures and measuring spoons for accurate measuring
- 8 - 12 cup ceramic, glass, aluminum or plastic bowl for mixing ingredients
- Smaller bowls to proof yeast, to mix glazes, etc.
- Electric mixer to beat light batters
- Heavy mixer or food processor to mix or knead heavy or sticky dough
- Balloon whisk for beating liquid batters
- Wooden spoon for mixing in flour
- Rolling pin for shaping dough
- Plastic dough scraper to scrape bowl and keep work surface clean
- Knife to cut dough
- Pastry brush for brushing on glazes
- Baking pans and sheets. These vary according to your recipe but try to use good quality, fairly heavy aluminum or stainless steel pans for best results
- Cooling racks for cooling baked loaves and rolls
- Oven for baking
- Oven mitts (long mitts protect arms and wrists from burns when handling hot pans)

# *Techniques*

## Mixing and Kneading

In yeast doughs, the gluten in the wheat flour needs to be developed so your bread or rolls will rise properly as the yeast gives off carbon dioxide. To do this the batter must first be beaten and then the thicker dough kneaded. Kneading is a technique that takes practise but produces a product well worth the learning. The best place for kneading is a counter or table-top that is a height convenient for your arms to be fully extended, palms of hands flat on the top. You can start

### *To knead*

- With floured hands, fold the dough in half toward you.
- Push it away with the heels of both hands with a rolling or rocking motion.
- Give dough a quarter turn and repeat the process again. Fold - push - turn again and again until the dough is smooth and elastic. This will take approximately 10 minutes depending on the recipe. Don't be gentle with the dough — it needs a good working to develop properly. Sticky dough will be uncovered occasionally during kneading; sprinkle with flour and keep going. The dough will look smooth and feel springy and soft when it is properly kneaded.

kneading the dough in the bowl, working the remaining flour into it with your hands. When you have a rough, shaggy mass roll it onto your lightly-floured work surface.

## Rising

After kneading, dough needs time to rise in a warm place.
- Place a ball of kneaded dough in a large clean bowl that has been greased with vegetable oil. The bowl can be warmed beforehand by rinsing with hot water and then thoroughly dried to aid rising.

- Cover bowl loosely with plastic wrap.
- Place bowl in a warm place (80 - 85° F) away from drafts.You can do this by setting dough in an unheated oven with a large pan of hot water under it or by setting the bowl in a pan of warm, but not hot, water or just by putting it in a sunny spot on the counter.

Dough needs to rise until it is "double in bulk." To test for this, lightly press two fingers into the dough about 1/2 an inch, near the edge of the bowl. If the indentations remain, the dough is ready for the next step. A yeast batter cannot be tested this way, but it will appear bubbly when it has doubled in bulk.

## Punching down

After the first rise the dough must be punched down so you can work with it. Push your fist into the centre of the dough and pull the sides into the middle all the way around to form a smaller ball, smooth it out and turn the ball over. Some doughs will be left to rise again. This second rising gives an even finer textured product but most doughs are ready to be shaped after only a 5 - 10 minute rest.

## Shaping and Panning

Breads and rolls can be formed into a variety of shapes — follow directions given in your recipe.

For regular loaves, divide dough in equal pieces depending on how much flour is used and the number indicated by the recipe. Press or roll each piece into a flat oval approximately the size of your loaf pan. Fold it in half towards you and pinch the seam together tightly, tucking in the ends. Place your loaf, seam-side down, in a greased pan. (Greasing with shortening works better than vegetable oil to prevent sticking.) The loaf should fill the pan half to two-thirds full.

Rolls are usually shaped into balls the size of a large egg or golf ball. Cut pieces of dough from the larger mass. Pinch each piece to a centre point on the bottom of the roll, creating a smooth top surface.

There are all kinds of pans and containers used in bread making, from baking sheets to casseroles to tin cans. It is important to remember to divide your dough as evenly as possible to ensure even baking and an attractive finished product. If using glass or dark-coloured pans, remember to decrease your oven temperature by approximately 25° as these pans hold the heat. The most common size of loaf pan used today is a 9 x 5 x 3 inch pan. Regular baking sheets can be used for hearth-style loaves, braided loaves, etc., as the recipe indicates and can also be used for a crustier style roll. Softer rolls or pan buns are baked in a 9 x 13 x 2 inch pan. Muffin tins also make nicely-shaped individual rolls and petit brioches.

## Second Rise

After panning, the dough needs a second rise until double in bulk. This usually takes 45 to 60 minutes. Place pans in a warm place, cover loosely with plastic wrap or a damp tea

towel. A general rule of thumb is to keep a close eye on your loaves. Once they have risen an inch over the top of the pan they are ready for baking regardless of the rising time elapsed.

## Baking

Preheat your oven to the specified temperature before putting your pans in. Place the pans in the centre of the oven leaving at least two inches between pans so the heat circulates around them. Products on baking sheets turn out better baked one sheet at a time. It is during the first ten to fifteen minutes of baking that the dough rises to its maximum and forms its final baked shape, so it is best not to disturb it during this time. This process is called "oven spring." After oven spring occurs, keep an eye on your loaves for even browning; the pans may need to be turned part way through baking to ensure this.

## When is it Done?

Testing for doneness is accomplished by tapping the bottom or side of your loaf with a knuckle — if the loaf sounds hollow, it is done. If the loaf is soft or sounds soft, it is not fully baked and needs to be returned to the oven for additional baking.

Quick breads can be tested for doneness with a slender metal probe or wooden toothpick — if the probe inserted into the centre comes out clean, your product is done; if it comes out with moist crumbs attached it needs further baking.

## Cooling

To prevent sogginess, breads and rolls should be removed from their pans as soon as they come out of the oven. They should be cooled completely on wire racks before storing.

## Storing, Freezing and Freshening

Breads can be stored in plastic bags or wrapped well with plastic wrap. Bread stored in plastic at room temperature will be moister than bread stored in a bread box, uncovered, which retains its crispness. To freeze, wrap loaves in plastic bags or wrap or aluminum foil, remove air and seal well. Frozen loaves will keep up to three months. Thaw breads in their original wrapper at room temperature for 2 - 3 hours, then wrap in foil and reheat in a 350° F oven for about 15 minutes. (Remove or open the foil for the last 5 minutes to crisp the crust.) If desired, foil-wrapped breads can be completely thawed in the oven — place the loaf in a 350° F oven for 15 to 30 minutes.

## Cool Rise Method

Use of this method means dough can be prepared one day and then baked later that day or the next day. This method can be used for almost any bread recipe. Dough is prepared according to recipe directions, then left to rest for about 30 minutes. It is shaped and placed in greased pans. The pans are loosely covered with plastic wrap allowing room for the dough to rise. The pans are then refrigerated from 2 to 24 hours. The dough will continue to rise as it cools, but the cold retards the yeast action, slowing it down. When you are ready to bake, remove the pans from the refrigerator and let stand at room temperature for 10 -15 minutes before baking as directed in the recipe.

## Let's Get Baking!

All of this information may seem daunting to you now, but after working with the dough and baking a few loaves you will begin to get a feel for the dough and the techniques. Remember, home-baked breads do not have to be perfect or look perfect to taste good. All bakers occasionally make less than perfect products and practise helps. It may take some time and patience but it's well worth the effort — after all who can resist the delicious aroma and flavour of freshly baked bread. Enjoy the learning process, and good baking to you!

# *Recipes*

Many recipes in this book use the "Quick Mix" or no-dissolve yeast method — please be sure you are using yeast that works properly in this process (read your yeast package instructions). If not, substitute the Traditional Water Dissolve method. After dissolving yeast, add remaining ingredients and 1 to 1 1/2 cups flour. Beat together until smooth. Add remaining flour as called for in the recipe and continue to follow recipe directions.

## Air Buns

### Traditional Yeast Method

This delicious bun recipe probably has its origins in a number of places and comes from bakers of many backgrounds experimenting with new ingredients and methods looking for the perfect product. Wherever it comes from, it is a great recipe for beginners because it seems to turn out every time.

| | |
|---|---|
| 1 Tbsp. | *active dry yeast* |
| 1 Tbsp. | *sugar* |
| 1/2 cup | *lukewarm water* |
| 1/2 cup | *sugar* |
| 1/2 cup | *shortening* |
| 1 tsp. | *salt* |
| 2 Tbsps | *vinegar* |
| 4 cups | *lukewarm water* |
| 8 - 10 cups | *all purpose flour* |

1) Combine yeast, 1 Tbsp. sugar, 1/2 cup water and let stand 10 minutes.
2) Combine sugar, shortening, salt and vinegar, beat with electric mixer until well blended.
3) Add yeast and 3 - 4 cups flour, blend in and then beat until well mixed. Add remaining flour a cup at a time and mix with wooden spoon until dough is not sticky.
4) Remove dough to a floured surface and knead 10 minutes.
5) Return dough to clean, lightly-greased bowl, turning to grease the top. Cover and let rise 2 hours in a warm place.
6) Punch dough down, cover and let rise another hour.
7) Punch down and remove dough from the bowl. Using a sharp knife, cut dough into pieces and form into small buns. Place on baking sheets about 2" apart.

8) Let rise in a warm place, 1 - 2 hours or until they are filling the pan.

9) Bake at 400° F for 15 - 20 minutes. Remove from pans and cool completely on wire racks.

Makes six dozen.

**Easy White Bread**

## Traditional yeast method

Another good recipe to learn on, this recipe is also the result of experimentation with new ingredients and methods. It speeds up time from preparation to finished product and you only have to knead for 1 minute. It will give you a feel for the techniques and the properties of a yeast dough and best of all it tastes great when finished.

| | |
|---|---|
| *2 1/2 cups* | *warm water* |
| *2 packages* | *active dry yeast* |
| *1/2 cup* | *instant non-fat dry milk* |
| *2 Tbsps* | *sugar* |
| *2 tsps* | *salt* |
| *1/3 cup* | *vegetable oil* |
| *6 - 7 cups* | *all purpose flour* |

1) Place warm water in a large mixing bowl and sprinkle yeast over the top. Let stand until yeast dissolves.

2) Add dry milk, sugar, vegetable oil and 3 cups of the flour, blend well with an electric mixer or by hand. Increase mixer speed to medium and beat for 3 minutes, scraping down the sides of the bowl occasionally. (If mixing by hand, beat vigorously for 3 minutes).

3) Remove mixer from bowl and stir in remaining flour using a wooden spoon and then by hand until a rough, stiff dough forms.

4) Turn the dough onto a lightly-floured surface, cover with a towel and let rest for 15 minutes.

5) Knead the dough about 1 minute until smooth. Cut the dough in half with a sharp knife, form these halves into balls and let rest 4-5 minutes.

6) Shape the balls into loaves by pressing the dough into a flat oval almost the size of your pan (9" x 5" loaf pans). Fold the oval in half lengthwise, seal the seam tightly and tuck in the ends.

7) Place loaves, seam-side down into the loaf pans. Cover, let rise in a warm place about 45 minutes or until the dough is about 1" above the edge of the pan.

8) Preheat oven to 400°F, bake loaves for 10 minutes.Reduce heat to 350°F and bake another 35 minutes. Test for doneness — if the loaves sound hollow when rapped remove from pans and place on wire racks to cool. If not,return to the oven for an additional 5-10 minutes.

Makes two loaves.

### Anadama Bread

*Quick mix yeast method*

When settlers came to the Americas hundreds of years ago they found ground corn being used by the native peoples in many areas. Being the pioneers they were, these women soon incorporated cornmeal into the recipes they brought from home. This recipe, Anadama Bread, has a number of stories attached to its name. In one, a New England backwoodsman, finally tired of his usual cornmeal and molasses porridge, calls to his wife: "Anna, dammit, this is what I want," while mixing flour and yeast into his porridge. The fine-textured cornmeal bread with a light taste of molasses is sure to have pleased him as it will you and your family.

| | |
|---|---|
| 5 - 6 cups | all purpose flour |
| 2 1/2 tsps | salt |
| 1 cup | yellow cornmeal |
| 2 pkgs | active dry yeast |
| 1/4 cup | margarine or butter, at room temperature |
| 2 cups | hot water |
| 1/3 cup | molasses |

1) In a large bowl stir together 2 1/2 cups of the flour, plus the salt, cornmeal and yeast. Add margarine.

2) In a bowl combine water and molasses, stir together. Gradually pour the molasses mixture into the dry ingredients and beat 2 minutes with an electric mixer at medium speed. Add enough flour to make a thick batter, (about 1/2 cup) and beat at high speed for 2 minutes, scraping the sides of the bowl occasionally.

3) Stir in the rest of the flour with a wooden spoon and work with your hands as the dough stiffens. When the dough is soft but no longer sticky, turn it out onto a lightly - floured surface.

4) Knead the dough until it is smooth and elastic (about 8 minutes).

5) Place dough in a greased bowl, turning to coat the top. Cover and place in a warm, draft-free place, until it doubles in bulk (about 50 minutes).

6) Punch down the dough and cut in 2 pieces with a sharp knife. With the hands, form each into an oval approximately the length of your pan (9" x 5" loaf pan). Fold in half lengthwise, pinch the seam tightly and tuck in the ends. Place seam-side down in the loaf pans.

7) Cover the pans and let dough rise about 45 minutes or until the loaves have risen about 1" above the edge of the pan.

8) Preheat the oven to 375°F. Bake loaves for 45 minutes. When the loaves have a golden crust, test for doneness. If the loaves give a hollow sound when rapped, remove from pans and cool on wire racks.

Makes two loaves.

## Corn Bubbleloaf

### *Quick Mix yeast method*

This recipe uses the "Cold Dough" method and is baked in a tube pan (a round pan with a tube in the centre of it). It is fun to serve with its very unusual bread shape and is delicious to eat.

| | | |
|---|---|---|
| 5 - 6 | *cups all purpose flour* | *(1.35-1.6 kg)* |
| 2 Tbsps | *sugar* | *(30 mL)* |
| 1 Tbsp. | *salt* | *(15 mL)* |
| 1 cup | *yellow cornmeal* | *(250 mL)* |
| 2 pkgs | *active dry yeast* | |
| 1 3/4 cups | *milk* | *(325 mL)* |
| 1 cup | *water* | *(250 mL)* |
| 3 Tbsps | *margarine or butter* | *(45 mL)* |
| | *vegetable oil* | |
| | *melted margarine or butter* | |

1) In a large bowl thoroughly mix 1 1/2 cups flour, plus the sugar, salt, cornmeal and undissolved active dry yeast.
2) Combine milk, water and 3 Tbsps margarine in a sauce pan, heat over low heat until liquids are hot to the touch. Gradually add to the dry ingredients and beat 2 minutes with the electric mixer at medium speed, scraping the bowl occasionally.
3) Add 1/2 cup flour and beat at medium speed 1 minute, scraping the bowl occasionally. Using a wooden spoon, stir in enough flour to make a soft dough. Turn out onto a lightly-floured surface.
4) Knead dough 8 to 10 minutes until smooth and elastic. Cover with plastic wrap and a tea towel and let rest for 20 minutes.
5) Punch dough down, cut into 32 equal pieces. On a lightly floured surface shape into balls. Arrange the balls in a greased 10 inch tube pan, making 2 layers.

Brush loaf with vegetable oil and cover loosely with plastic wrap leaving room for the dough to rise slightly. Refrigerate for 2 to 24 hours.

6) When ready to bake, remove the dough from the refrigerator. Uncover carefully and let stand for 10 minutes at room temperature. Puncture any gas bubbles with a greased toothpick.

7) Preheat oven to 375°F. Bake loaf for 40 - 45 minutes. When baked remove carefully from the pan and cool on a wire rack. Brush the top with melted margarine to give a soft crust, if desired.

Makes one large loaf.

## Tortillas

The tortilla is a traditional Mexican bread, resembling a thin, round, unleavened pancake. It has been served in Mexico for many centuries. Even before the Spaniards arrived and introduced wheat and wheat flour, tortillas were made from "masa" or ground corn. Nowadays those who make their own tortillas can use "masa harina" (corn flour), wheat flour or as in this recipe a mixture of all-purpose flour and cornmeal.

| | |
|---|---|
| 1 1/2 cups | all-purpose flour |
| 1 cup | cornmeal |
| 1/2 tsp. | salt |
| 1 1/4 cups | water |

1) Blend together the flour, cornmeal and salt. Stir in just enough water so the mixture forms a ball of dough.
2) Place dough onto a lightly-floured surface. Knead and pound dough until it is smooth and elastic.
3) Cover ball of dough with a damp tea towel and let it rest for 10 minutes.
4) Cut dough into 1-inch balls and roll each into thin 5 to 6 -inch circles. (use larger balls for larger tortillas.) This canbe done either with a heavy rolling pin or by placing the ball of dough between 2 pieces of waxed paper and pressing it out with a heavy pan or pie plate.
5) Bake tortillas on a heated skillet or cast iron fry pan. Turn tortillas so that both sides are flecked with brown.
6) When done, flip tortillas out onto a warm platter or baking sheet and keep them in a warm oven until all are baked.
7) Serve with your favourite meat or salad filling or use to make enchiladas or burritos.

Makes 12-14.

## Barm Brack

### Quick Mix yeast method

This recipe makes a light, fruit-filled loaf traditional to Irish baking. Its name, "Barm Brack" literally means "yeast bread" in Irish Gaelic. It is one of the few examples of an Irish yeast loaf and is delicious served with a thick spreading of butter.

| | |
|---|---|
| 4 1/2 to 5 1/2 cups | all-purpose flour |
| 1/2 cup | sugar |
| 1 1/2 tsps | salt |
| 1 tsp. | grated lemon peel |
| 3 pkgs. | active dry yeast |
| 1 1/4 cups | water |
| 1/2 cup | milk |
| 1/4 cup | margarine |
| 2 | eggs, room temperature |
| 1 1/4 cups | raisins |
| 1/3 cup | chopped mixed candied fruits |

1) In a large bowl thoroughly mix 1 cup flour, with the sugar, salt, lemon peel and undissolved yeast.
2) Combine water, milk and margarine in a saucepan. Heat over low heat until liquid is hot to the touch. Gradually add to dry ingredients and beat 2 minutes with an electric mixer at medium speed or vigorously with a wooden spoon, scraping the bowl occasionally.
3) Add eggs and 1/2 cup flour, enough to make a thick batter. Beat at medium speed 1 minute. With a wooden spoon, stir in enough additional flour to make a soft dough.
4) Add raisins and fruits and work these in by hand while the dough is in the bowl. Turn out onto a lightly-floured surface.

5) Knead dough until smooth and elastic, about 8 to 10 minutes. Place in a greased bowl, turn dough to grease the top. Cover; let rise in a warm, draft-free place until doubled in bulk (about 60 minutes).
6) Punch dough down and turn out onto a lightly-floured surface. Divide in half and shape into loaves. Place into greased 9" x 5" loaf pans. Cover and let rise in a warm, draft-free place until double in bulk (about 50 minutes or until the dough is 1" above the side of the pan).
7) Bake at 375°F for 30 to 35 minutes, or until done. If loaves are browning too quickly, cover with foil. When baked, remove from pans and cool on wire racks.

Makes two loaves

## Irish Soda Bread

This is an example of a quick bread and therefore does not use yeast as a leavener but baking powder and baking soda. This is the more popular method for traditional Irish bread and couldn't be left out.

| | |
|---|---|
| *1 1/2 cups* | *buttermilk* |
| *2 Tbsps* | *butter or margarine, melted* |
| *1* | *large egg, lightly beaten* |
| *1 1/2 cups* | *seedless raisins or currants* |
| *3 cups* | *all purpose flour* |
| *2/3 cup* | *sugar* |
| *1 Tbsp.* | *baking powder* |
| *1 tsp.* | *baking soda* |
| *1 tsp.* | *salt* |

1) Preheat oven to 350°F. Grease a 9" x 5" loaf pan and set aside.
2) Place buttermilk, melted margarine, egg and raisins in a medium bowl.
3) Combine dry ingredients in a large bowl and mix thoroughly.

4) Add buttermilk mixture to dry ingredients and mix until combined. Spoon into the prepared pan.
5) Bake 50 to 55 minutes, test for doneness by rapping with the knuckles, loaf should sound hollow. Leave in the pan for 1 minute, then remove and cool completely on a wire rack.

Makes one loaf.

## Hot Cross Buns

### Traditional yeast method

These lightly-spiced, fruit-filled rolls are best known as an English delicacy served at Easter celebrations. In fact, their origins go back much farther to more pagan times. The cross cut in the top of each bun can symbolize the 4 quarters of the moon, and buns similar to these were offered as sacrifices to gods and goddesses in Egyptian and Saxon times and by ancient Aztecs and Incas. In the early days of the Christian Church, Hot Cross Buns were adopted by the British for their own Good Friday services.

| | |
|---|---|
| 2 pkgs | active dry yeast |
| 1/2 cup | warm water |
| 1/2 cup | lukewarm milk (scalded then cooled) |
| 3/4 cup | lukewarm mashed potatoes |
| 1/2 cup | sugar |
| 1 tsp. | salt |
| 1/2 cup | margarine, softened |
| 2 | eggs |
| 3/4 tsp. | cinnamon |
| 1/4 tsp. | nutmeg |
| 1 cup | raisins |
| 1/2 cup | mixed candied fruit, finely chopped |
| 4 1/2 cups | all purpose flour |
| | Egg Glaze |
| | Confectioners' Icing (Recipe follows) |

1) In a large bowl, dissolve yeast in warm water. Let stand for five minutes. Stir in milk, mashed potatoes, sugar, salt, margarine, eggs, spices, fruits and 2 1/2 cups of flour.Beat until smooth.
2) Mix in remaining flour to form a soft dough.
3) Turn the dough out onto a lightly-floured surface and knead about 5 minutes until dough is smooth and elastic.
4) Place into a greased bowl, turning once to coat the top of the dough. Cover and let rise in a warm place about 1 1/2 hours or until double in bulk.
5) Punch dough down, divide in half. Using a sharp knife, cut each half into 16 equal pieces. Shape into smooth balls and place about 2" apart on greased baking sheets.
6) With scissors or a sharp knife, cut a cross on the top of each bun. Cover and let rise until double in bulk, about40 minutes.
7) Preheat oven to 375˚F. Brush the top of buns with egg glaze (1 egg yolk mixed with 2 Tbsps cold water). Bake about 20 minutes or until golden brown.
8) Remove from pans and cool on wire racks.
9) When cool, buns can be frosted with Confectioners' icing, if desired.

### Confectioners' Icing

Beat together 1 cup confectioners' or icing sugar, 1 Tbsp milk and 1/2 tsp vanilla until smooth and spreadable.

Makes 32 rolls.

## French Bread

### Traditional Yeast method

Today many bakers in France still rise before dawn to make those special long loaves of bread we know as French bread: slender "baguette," or the plump "pain de menage." They still bake it in the time-honoured way — first in a steamy, moist atmosphere and then in dry heat to crisp the crust — that makes French loaves like no other. Because of this special baking process and because the local "boulangerie" is likely close at hand to provide his delicious loaves fresh everyday, few French families bake their own bread. This recipe allows us to try to duplicate at home those wonderful loaves. Bon Chance!

| | |
|---|---|
| 2 cups | *warm water* |
| 1 pkg. | *active dry yeast* |
| 1 Tbsp. | *salt* |
| 2 tsps | *sugar* |
| 1 Tbsp. | *margarine, softened* |
| 5 1/2 - 6 cups | *all purpose flour* |
| | *Cornmeal* |

1) Place warm water in a large bowl and sprinkle yeast over the top. Stir until the yeast is dissolved.
2) Add salt, sugar, margarine and 2 cups of flour; beat with either an electric mixer or with a wooden spoon until smooth (about 2 minutes).
3) Gradually mix in remaining flour by hand until the dough leaves the sides of the bowl.
4) Turn dough out onto a lightly-floured surface and knead about 10 minutes until the dough is smooth and elastic. Dough will be somewhat stiff.
5) Place dough into a greased bowl, turning to grease the top. Cover and let rise in a warm, draft-free place about 1 1/2 hours until it is double in bulk.

6) Punch down; turn out of the bowl and divide into thirds.

7) Roll out each third into a 13 x 9 inch oblong. On the wideside roll the dough up tightly like a jelly roll, tuck in endsand pinch the seam tightly to seal.

8) Place the loaves, 3 inches apart, on a large, greased baking sheet that has been sprinkled with cornmeal.Brush each loaf with cold water. With scissors or a sharpknife, cut 4 diagonal slashes across the top of each loaf.

9) Let rise, uncovered, in a warm, draft-free place about 1 1/2 hours, until double in bulk.

10)Preheat oven to 400°F. About 5 minutes before putting loaves in, place a shallow pan of hot water on oven bottom or lowest shelf. Brush or spray (using an atomizer) loaves with water before placing in the hot, moist oven. Spray or brush the loaves every 5 minutes for the first 20 minutesof baking. When doing this don't pull the loaves out of the oven or you will lose the moist air inside. After 20 minutes remove the shallow pan of water and let the loaves finish baking in a dry oven for another 20-25 minutes until loaves are golden brown and sound hollow when rapped.

11)Remove loaves from the pan and cool completely on wire racks.

Makes three loaves.

**Brioche**

## Quick Mix yeast method

This bread with its butter-rich flavour and fine texture stands out among the delicious egg breads produced in Europe. This french loaf is almost a cross between a cake and a bread. The name "brioche," pronounced "bree-oshe," comes from the old French words "bris" (break) and "hacher" (stir) and relates to the butter that is broken down from its hard form and stirred or mixed into the dough. Brioche is fairly easy to make if you have a heavy duty mixer although it can be made by hand. The dough is soft and moist — it must stay as cold as possible throughout preparation to prevent the butter separating from the dough. Brioche can be baked in classic brioche molds, either fluted or plain; in petit brioche or muffin tins or simply in ordinary loaf pans.

| | |
|---|---|
| 4 1/2 cups | all-purpose flour |
| 1 pkg. | active dry yeast |
| 1/4 cup | sugar |
| 1 tsp. | salt |
| 1/2 cup | hot water |
| 6 | eggs, at room temperature |
| 1 cup | unsalted butter, |
| | cut into small pieces and softened |
| | Egg Glaze |

1) In the bowl of a heavy-duty mixer fitted with a paddle attachment, combine 1 cup flour, yeast, sugar, and salt.Add hot water and beat at medium speed for 2 minutes oruntil smooth. If you are working by hand use a regularmixer at this stage.
2) Add eggs one at a time, beating well after each addition. Gradually add 2 cups more flour.

3) When well blended, add butter a few pieces at a time. Beat just until completely incorporated. Gradually add exactly1 1/2 cups more flour slowly at low speed for about 2 minutes. Beat until thoroughly blended and creamy. If you are not using the heavy duty mixer you will have todo this by hand. The dough will be very soft and sticky.

4) Scrape with a spatula into a greased bowl. Cover tightly with plastic wrap and let rise at a cool room temperature until doubled in bulk (about 3 hours).

5) Gently punch down dough with a spatula, cover tightly and refrigerate 12 hours or overnight.

6) Turn chilled dough out onto a lightly-floured surface. Divide dough into 4 equal pieces. Roll each piece into a rope about 12 inches long and 1 inch in diameter. Divideeach into 4, two-inch pieces and 4, one-inch pieces.Round pieces with fingers to make 16 larger ballsand 16 smaller balls. Don't worry if the balls vary in sizesomewhat. Place larger balls in well-buttered 3 1/2 inch fluted molds or regular muffin tins. Snip an "X" on the topof each with kitchen scissors. Now push your fingerthrough the middle of the dough to the bottom. Place the small topknot in each centre. Brush with egg glaze (1 egg yolk beaten together with 1 Tbsp. milk).

7) Let rise at a cool room temperature until doubled in bulk (about 45 minutes). If this dough is allowed to rise in a traditional warm temperature the butter will separate from the rest of the dough.

8) Bake in a preheated 400°F. oven for 10 to 15 minutes or until golden brown. Remove from molds to cool completely on wire racks.

Brioche are best eaten after they have been reheated.
Makes 16 rolls.

## Stollen

### Quick Mix Yeast Method

Serving this fruit and nut-filled bread is a German Christmas tradition. Families gather together on Christmas Eve to eat the delicious "Christ Stollen" before attending church. The loaves are also served to guests throughout the Christmas season in place of fruit cake.

| | |
|---|---|
| 5 1/2 - 6 1/2 cups | all purpose flour |
| 1/2 cup | sugar |
| 1 1/4 tsps | salt |
| 2 pkgs | active dry yeast |
| 3/4 cup | milk |
| 1 cup | water |
| 2/3 cup | margarine, softened |
| 3 | eggs, room temperature |
| 3/4 cup | blanched almonds, chopped |
| 3/4 cup | mixed candied fruits |
| 1/3 cup | golden raisins |
| | Confectioners' icing |
| | Candied cherry halves (optional) |
| | Whole almonds (optional) |

1) In a large bowl, thoroughly mix 1 1/2 cups flour, sugar, salt and yeast.
2) Combine milk, water, and margarine in a saucepan. Heat over low heat until liquids are hot to the touch. Gradually add to dry ingredients and beat 2 minutes with an electric mixer at medium speed, or beat vigorously with a wooden spoon, scraping the bowl occasionally.
3) Add eggs and 1/2 cup flour. Beat at medium speed 1 minute, scraping the bowl. With a mixing spoon, stir in enough additional flour to make a soft dough. Turn dough out on to a lightly-floured surface.
4) Knead dough until smooth and elastic, about 8 to 10 minutes. Knead in blanched almonds, candied fruit and raisins.
5) Place in a greased bowl, turning to grease the top. Cover and let rise in a warm, draft-free place, until doubled in bulk, about 1 1/2 hours.
6) Punch dough down; turn out onto a lightly-flouredsurface. With a sharp knife cut dough into 3 equal pieces. Roll each piece into a 12 x 7 inch oval. Fold the oval lengthwise in half; press firmly only on the folded edge and don't tuck in the ends of the loaves. Place the stollen on greased baking sheets. Cover and let rise in a warm place until doubled in bulk, about 45 minutes.
7) Bake at 350°F. for 20 to 25 minutes, or until hollow when rapped. Remove from pans and place on wire racks.
8) Frost with Confectioners' Icing while the loaves are warm. If desired, decorate the loaves with cherry halves and almonds.

## *Confectioners' Icing*

Beat together 1 1/2 cups icing sugar, 1 1/2 Tbsps milk and 1/2 tsp. almond extract until mixture is smooth and has a creamy consistency.
Makes three.

## German Rye Bread

### Quick Mix Yeast Method

Rye flour is a dark grain flour milled from rye, one of the most important European cereal grains. Rye bread recipes abound all over Europe, Scandinavia and the Slavic countries. There are 4 kinds of rye flour: white, medium, dark and rye meal or pumpernickel. The most commonly used is medium, the purest form of rye flour. This German recipe uses cocoa to give the loaves a darker, richer colouring, with little or no taste remaining after the loaves are baked. It is a combination of medium rye flour and white all-purpose flour.

| | |
|---|---|
| 3 cups | all purpose flour |
| 3 cups | rye flour |
| 2 pkgs | active dry yeast |
| 1/4 cup | cocoa |
| 1 Tbsp. | sugar |
| 1 Tbsp. | salt |
| 1 Tbsp. | caraway seed (optional) |
| 2 cups | hot water |
| 1/3 cup | molasses |
| 2 Tbsps | shortening, softened |

1) In a large mixing bowl, measure 1 1/2 cups all-purpose flour, 1 1/2 cups rye flour, yeast, cocoa, sugar, salt and caraway seeds. Mix thoroughly to blend the ingredients.
2) Pour in the water, molasses and soft shortening. Beat with the electric mixer or by hand slowly for 30 seconds and then at high speed for 3 minutes. The dough will be thick and elastic and will pull away from the sides of the bowl.

3) Gradually add flour, 1/2 cup at a time alternating both white and rye, until the dough is a soft mass and is no longer moist and sticky. Turn out onto a lightly-floured surface.

4) Knead the dough for approximately 5 minutes. The dough may be somewhat sticky because of the high rye content. Scrape it off the counter top with a spatula or scraper. Add a bit more flour to the dough and keep your hands lightly dusted. As you keep kneading it will become a soft, velvety dough.

5) When finished cover the dough with a towel or piece of waxed paper and let it rest for about 20 minutes.

6) Punch down and with a sharp knife cut the dough in half. Shape each piece into a round ball and flatten slightly for round loaves. For a long loaf, roll the piece into an 8 x 15inch rectangle. Roll up tightly, seal the seam and tuck in the ends. Place on a greased baking sheet.

7) Brush the loaves with vegetable oil, cover loosely with plastic wrap to allow for slight rising. Place the baking sheet in the refrigerator, leave for 2 to 24 hours.

8) When ready to bake allow the loaves to stand at room temperature for 10 minutes. Preheat the oven to 400°F. With a sharp knife or scissors cut a cross (X) on round loaves and diagonal slashes on long loaves just before baking.

9) Place in the oven and bake for 30 to 40 minutes. Test for doneness, if fully baked, remove from the oven. Remove loaves from baking sheets and cool completely on wire racks.

Makes two loaves.

**Panettone**

## Traditional Yeast Method

Citron, raisins and currants grace this delicious Italian loaf. Panettone originally came from Milan but now most Italian regions have their own versions. Panettone is served at Christmas time as well as Easter, weddings and other special occasions.

| | |
|---|---|
| 2 pkgs | active dry yeast |
| 1 cup | warm water |
| 1/2 cup | milk (scalded then cooled) |
| 1/2 cup | sugar |
| 1 tsp. | salt |
| 1/2 cup | margarine |
| 3 eggs | (room temperature) |
| 5 -6 cups | all purpose flour |
| 1/2 cup | citron, chopped |
| 1/2 cup | seedless raisins |
| | OR 1/4 cup raisins and 1/4 cup currants |
| 2 Tbsps | slivered almonds |
| | OR 2 Tbsp pinon (pine) nuts |
| 1 Tbsp. | anise seeds |
| 1 | egg |
| 1 Tbsp. | water |

1) In a large bowl, dissolve yeast in 1/2 cup water in which 1/2 tsp. sugar has been dissolved. Stir in remaining water, milk, sugar, salt, margarine and 3 eggs. Add 3 cups of flour and beat by hand or with the electric mixer until smooth (about 2 minutes). Scrape the sides of the bowl occasionally.

2) With a wooden spoon, stir in fruits, nuts, anise seeds and enough remaining flour to make a soft dough. Turn the dough out onto a lightly-floured surface.

3) Knead for 8 to 10 minutes until the dough is smooth and elastic. Place into a greased bowl, turning to coat the top. Cover and let rise in a warm, draft-free place until double in bulk, about 1 hour.

4) Punch dough down, cover and let rise again about 30 minutes, until almost double.

5) Punch down again and turn out onto a lightly-floured surface. With a sharp knife cut dough in half and form into round balls, flattening slightly.

6) Place balls at opposite corners of a greased baking sheet. With a sharp knife, cut a cross (X) 1/2 an inch deep on the top of each loaf.

7) Cover, let rise in a warm, draft-free place until double in bulk, about 1 hour.

8) Make an egg glaze by beating together 1 egg and 1 Tbsp. water, brush on top of each loaf.

9) Bake 35 to 45 minutes in a 350°F oven. When baked, remove from the baking sheet and cool completely on wire racks.

Makes two loaves.

## Pizza Crust

### *Traditional Yeast Method*

Pizza is an Italian specialty that most North Americans have come to enjoy. The word "pizza" literally means "pie" in Italian. In Italy, pizzerias everywhere bake their own regional specialties in wood-fired brick ovens. This gives them their unique texture and flavour that is hard to copy here at home. We are most familiar with Neapolitan-style pizza, a thin crust covered with tomatoes or tomato sauce, herbs and cheese. This recipe for pizza crust gives a thin, bread-like crust that you can top with your favourite ingredients.

| | |
|---|---|
| 3/4 cup | *lukewarm water* |
| 1 tsp. | *sugar* |
| 1 pkg. | *active dry yeast* |
| 2 cups | *all purpose flour* |
| 1/4 tsp. | *salt* |
| 2 Tbsps | *vegetable oil* |

1) Pour lukewarm water into a medium-sized bowl, add sugar; stir until dissolved. Sprinkle yeast over the top and let stand until foamy, about 10 minutes.
2) Meanwhile stir flour and salt together thoroughly. Set aside.
3) When yeast is ready, add oil and stir with a fork until blended. Slowly add yeast mixture to flour, mixing until dough starts to form a ball (this may not use all the yeast mixture).
4) Place dough on a lightly-floured board and knead 5 to 8 minutes until dough is smooth and shiny.
6) Place dough in a greased bowl, turning dough to coat the top, cover and let stand 15 minutes.
7) Preheat oven to 400°F. Place dough on lightly-floured surface and roll with a heavy rolling pin into a circle

about 1/4 to 1/2 an inch thick. Place in a lightly-greased, round pizza pan or on a greased baking sheet OR cut out 36, two- inch rounds and place on lightly-greased baking sheets.

8) Top the crust with your favourite tomato sauce and other ingredients.

9) Bake large pizza 15 to 20 minutes, mini pizzas 8 to 10 minutes. Large crust can also be baked untopped for 8 to 10 minutes, then reheated with toppings later.

Makes one large crust.

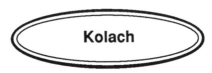

## Kolach

### *Traditional Yeast Method*

Kolach is a Ukrainian festive bread, featured at Christmas and other religious and family celebrations. It is a braided, ring-shaped bread. The name "Kolach" or "Kalach" is derived from the Ukrainian word "kolo" or circle. The circle is an ancient symbol of eternity in many cultures. At Christmas, three Kolach are stacked one atop the other and placed on a white cloth. A candle is inserted in the centre of the top loaf and burns throughout the evening meal. Kolach is a rich, delicious bread, excellent when eaten fresh or toasted.

| | |
|---|---|
| 1 Tbsp. | *active dry yeast* |
| 1 cup | *luke warm water* |
| 1 cup + 2 tsps | *sugar* |
| 4 | *cups water* |
| 3/4 cup | *margarine or butter, melted* |
| 1 tsp. | *salt* |
| 5 | *eggs, beaten* |
| 12 1/2 - 13 | *cups all-purpose flour* |

1) Dissolve yeast and 2 tsps sugar in 1 cup lukewarm water, let stand for 10 minutes.
2) Dissolve 1 cup sugar in 4 cups warm water, add melted margarine, salt and beaten eggs. Add yeast mixture and stir. Mix in 3 to 4 cups flour and beat with electric mixer until well blended.
3) Mix remaining flour in with a wooden spoon. Dough should be fairly stiff so braids will hold their shape. Turn dough out onto a lightly floured surface.
4) Knead dough until it is smooth and elastic, about 8 to 10 minutes. Cover and let rise in a warm, draft free place until double in bulk, about 1 hour.
5) Punch down and let rise again for 45 minutes.

## Shaping the Kolach

This recipe makes 3 round kolach, so the dough must be divided into 3 equal parts. Shape and bake each portion as directed.

1) Take 1/3 of the dough and divide it into 6 equal pieces. Take 2 of these pieces and roll them by hand into 24-inch-long strips.
2) Place the 2 strips side by side and starting at the centre, entwine the dough from left to right, repeat for the other end until you have a completely twisted strip.
3) Follow the same method for the remaining 4 portions of dough.
4) Place one braid into a well-greased 9-inch round cake pan, placing it around the outside edge and pinching its ends together gently.
5) Place the remaining braids side by side on the counter and entwine them from right to left making a double braid. Form them into a circle, trim ends and press dough together gently.

6) Place double braid on top of and in the centre of the braid in the pan. There will be a circular hole in the middle of the braids.
7) Cover and let rise in a warm place until double in bulk but not so long that the braids lose their shape.
8) Brush with a mixture of beaten egg and 2 Tbsps water. Bake at 350°F for 1 hour. Remove carefully from pan and cool on a wire rack.

Makes three loaves.

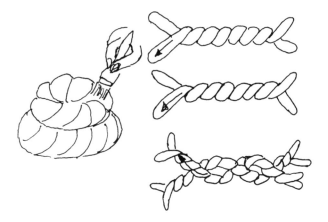

## Challah

### Quick Mix Yeast Method

"Challah" (pronounced "hal-la") is a delicious Jewish braided loaf that is fine textured and egg rich. In the preparation of these loaves, Jewish women may take a small part of the dough and burn it in the oven as an offering to God. The 2 braids served at the Sabbath meal honour the biblical forefathers who wandered for forty years in the desert and ate manna, or "bread from heaven."

| | |
|---:|:---:|
| 1 pkg. | active dry yeast |
| 5 cups | all purpose flour |
| 2 Tbsps | sugar |
| 1 1/2 tsps | salt |
| 1/3 cup | butter or margarine, softened |
| 1 cup | hot water |
| 1 pinch | saffron |
| 3 | eggs and |
| 1 | egg yolk, room temperature |

**Glaze**

| | |
|---:|:---:|
| 1 | egg yolk (from above) |
| 2 Tbsps | sugar |
| 1 tsp. | cold water |
| 1/2 tsp. | poppy seeds |

1) In a large bowl mix yeast, 2 cups flour, sugar, salt and butter or margarine. Gradually add hot water to dry ingredients and beat with electric mixer at medium speed for 2 minutes. Scrape the bowl occasionally.
2) Add saffron, 3 eggs and 1 egg white (reserving the yolk). The batter will be thick. Beat for 2 minutes at high speed. Set aside mixer and continue mixing flour with a wooden

spoon. Add about 3 additional cups of flour until you have a soft dough and it is no longer sticky.

3) Turn the dough out onto a lightly-floured surface and knead about 8 minutes until the dough is smooth and elastic.

4) Place dough in a greased bowl, turn to coat the top. Cover and let rise in a warm, draft-free place until dough has doubled in bulk, about 1 hour.

5) Punch dough down and knead out the bubbles. Using a sharp knife cut the dough in half.

6) To braid, cut each half into 3 equal pieces. Roll each piece into a 12-inch length by hand. Lay rolls side by side, start entwining the ropes from the middle and working to one end. Pinch the ends securely together, turn and entwine the other end. Repeat with the second piece.

7) Place the 2 braids on a baking sheet. Beat together remaining egg yolk, sugar and cold water. Carefully brush braids with the mixture. Sprinkle with poppy seeds.

8) Let the loaves rise for approximately 1 hour until double in bulk. Don't cover but place in a warm, draft-free place.

9) Preheat oven to 400°F. Bake until the braids test done when a toothpick inserted in the centre comes out clean and dry. The loaves will be shiny golden brown.

10) Remove bread from the oven. Carefully remove from baking sheet and cool on wire racks. Handle loaves with care until they have cooled completely.

Makes two loaves.

## Pitas (Flat Bread)

### Traditional Yeast Method

This flat bread has been baked in the Middle East for many centuries. It has few ingredients, a simple method and can be baked in an oven or on hot rocks by a campfire. The pockets that develop are great to stuff with salad, meats, or simply spread with butter.

| | |
|---|---|
| *1 pkg.* | *active dry yeast* |
| *1 1/4 cups* | *warm water* |
| *3 - 4 cups* | *all purpose flour* |
| *2 tsps* | *salt* |

1) In a mixing bowl, dissolve yeast in warm water. Let stand for 5 minutes. Stir in 2 cups of flour and the salt. Beat vigorously with the electric mixer for 3 minutes. Add additional flour, 1/2 a cup at a time, mixing first with a spoon, then with your hands. A rough, shaggy mass should develop.
2) Turn the dough out onto a lightly-floured surface. Knead until the dough is soft, about 8 minutes.
3) Divide the dough into 6 pieces and form each into a round ball. Using a rolling pin, flatten each ball into a circle about 4 to 5 inches in diameter and 1/4 inch thick. Alternatively, place ball between two pieces of waxed paper, then flatten with a pie plate.
4) Place the loaves together on the work surface and cover with a towel or wax paper. Let them rest for 45 minutes or until they are slightly puffy.

5) Preheat the oven to 500°F. Turn the rounds upside down onto a lightly-greased baking sheet. Bake for 15 to 18 minutes until they are light brown and puffed in the centre. Remove from pan and place on wire racks to cool. The breads will be hard when removed from the oven but the crust will soften and flatten as they cool. They should be used within a day as they soon lose their freshness. They freeze well.

## Man - T'ou

### *Traditional Yeast Method*

These unique rolls come from Northern China. Bread is not a staple of the Chinese diet but yeast rolls are served in several Northern regions. The Chinese cook their breads not by baking but by steaming them or frying on top of the stove.

| | |
|---|---|
| *3 1/4 cups* | *all purpose flour* |
| *1 1/4 cups* | *warm water* |
| *1 pkg.* | *active dry yeast* |

1) Place water in a medium-sized bowl, sprinkle in yeast and let stand until dissolved (about 5 minutes).
2) Slowly add flour to yeast mixture, stirring and then beating vigorously until dough forms and pulls away from the sides of the bowl.
3) Turn the dough out onto a lightly-floured surface and knead about 4 minutes.
4) Place dough into a greased bowl, turning to coat the top. Cover with waxed paper and a towel and let rise in a warm, draft free place about 1 1/2 hours.
5) Punch dough down, remove from the bowl and cut into 12 equal pieces with a sharp knife. Shape pieces into balls about 2 inches in diameter.

6) Place the balls about 2 inches apart on a piece of cheese-cloth that fits into your steamer. Let them rest for 10 minutes.
7) Place tray in steamer and steam over boiling water for 20 minutes.
8) Remove and serve warm.
Makes 12 buns.

**Oatmeal Bannock**

### Quick Mix (no dissolve) Yeast Method

This yeast bannock is a bread of Scotland, although the Gaelic word bannock actually means cake. Perhaps this refers to the round shape of the bread. Whatever the meaning, there are many hundreds of kinds of bannocks, all associated with special days on the Scottish calender. For example, one Scottish tale says if you eat a bannock on Halloween Eve your dreams that night will tell you what's in your future.

| | |
|---|---|
| *2 1/2 - 3 cups* | *all purpose flour* |
| *1/3 cup* | *sugar* |
| *1/2 tsp* | *salt* |
| *1 cup* | *uncooked old fashioned rolled oats* |
| *2 pkgs* | *active dry yeast* |
| *1/3 cup* | *milk* |
| *1 cup* | *water* |
| *1/4 cup* | *margarine* |
| *1* | *egg (at room temperature)* |

*1/2 cup currants (substitute raisins if desired)*

1) In a large bowl, combine 1/2 cup of the flour, the sugar, salt, rolled oats and yeast. Blend thoroughly.

2) In a saucepan, combine milk, water and margarine. Heat over low heat until liquids are hot to the touch. Gradually add to the dry ingredients and beat with an electric mixer for 2 minutes, scraping the sides of the bowl occasionally.

3) Add egg and 1/2 cup more flour. Beat one minute at medium speed.

4) With a wooden spoon, stir in additional flour, enough to make a soft dough.

5) Turn dough out onto a lightly-floured surface and knead for about 10 minutes until dough is smooth and elastic. Knead in currants.

6) Place dough in a greased bowl, turning once to coat the top. Cover and let rise in a warm, draft-free place about 45 minutes until double in bulk.

7) Punch dough down, turn out onto a lightly-floured surface. With a sharp knife divide dough in half. Roll each half into an 8-inch circle.

8) Place each round into a greased 8 or 9-inch round cake pan. With a sharp knife, score each round into 8 wedges (do not cut dough all the way through).

9) Cover and let rise in a warm, draft-free place about 30 minutes or until double in bulk.

10) Bake at 375° F for 20 minutes. Remove from pans and cool completely on wire racks.

Makes two cakes.

## Buttermilk Scones

*Quick bread method*

The word "scone" is derived from the Gaelic word "sgonn." Traditionally scones were baked on a griddle (a flat iron plate) hung over a smouldering peat fire. In olden times, Scottish soldiers never left the croft without their supply of oat flour and a griddle in their packs, so wherever they were, with the addition of a little water and a fire, they could bake up a scone and share it 'round. The scone has become a mainstay of British teatime practices.

| | |
|---|---|
| 2 1/4 cups | *all purpose flour* |
| 2 Tbsps | *sugar* |
| 2 1/2 tsps | *baking powder* |
| 1/2 tsp. | *baking soda* |
| 1/2 tsp. | *salt* |
| 1/2 cup | *cold butter or margarine,* |
| | *cut in small pieces* |
| 1/2 cup | *currants* |
| | *(substitute raisins if desired)* |
| 1 cup | *buttermilk* |
| 1 | *egg, beaten* |
| | *Milk* |
| | *granulated sugar* |

1) In a large bowl, combine flour, sugar, baking powder, soda and salt. Blend well.
2) Add butter or margarine to the dry ingredients. Using a pastry blender or 2 knives, cut in butter until mixture resembles coarse crumbs.
3) Stir in currants.
4) Add buttermilk and stir with a fork only until mixture is combined and forms a soft, moist dough.
5) Turn dough out onto a lightly-floured surface and knead with lightly-floured hands 8 to 10 times.
6) Divide dough into 2 equal portions. Pat or roll each portion into an 8-inch circle. Transfer circles to a greased baking sheet. Brush tops with milk and sprinkle with granulated sugar, if desired. Score the tops of each cake into 6 or 8 wedges.
7) Bake in a 425° F oven for 15 - 20 minutes until golden. Serve hot with butter and jam.

Makes 12

# Churros

Spain's bread is very much like the bread baked by its French neighbours: long, crusty loaves bought freshly-baked each day. Spaniards love their bread and consume it in great quantities. A favourite Spanish snack is the "churro" which is a deep-fried bread rolled in cinnamon and sugar, often served along with "coffee con leche" (milky coffee).

| | |
|---|---|
| *1/4 cup* | *butter or margarine,* |
| | *cut into small pieces* |
| *1/8 tsp.* | *salt* |
| *1 1/4 cups* | *all purpose flour, sifted* |
| *3* | *eggs* |
| *1/4 tsp.* | *vanilla extract* |
| | *Vegetable oil for frying* |
| *1/2 tsp.* | *cinnamon* |
| *1/2 cup* | *granulated sugar* |

1) In a deep skillet or deep fat fryer, slowly preheat vegetable oil (at least 1 1/2 inches) to 380° F.
2) In a medium saucepan over low heat, combine 1/2 cup water and the butter or margarine. Stir until butter is melted. Bring liquid just to boiling; add salt and remove from heat.
3) Add flour all at once and beat vigorously with a wooden spoon. Place pan over low heat and beat 2 minutes until batter is very smooth.
4) Remove from the heat and let batter cool slightly. Add eggs, 1 at a time, beating well after each addition.
5) Add vanilla and beat well until batter has a satin-like sheen.
6) Place batter into a large pastry bag with a large fluted tip, 1/2 inch wide. With wet scissors, cut batter into 2- inch strips as it drops into the fryer basket. Lower the basket quickly and carefully into the oil.

7) Deep fry churros a few at a time until they are golden brown, about 2 minutes per side. Lift them out and drain on paper towels.

8) Combine cinnamon and sugar in a medium bowl and toss drained churros in the mixture to coat well.

9) Serve warm.

Makes 24.

## St. Lucia Crown Loaf

### *Traditional Yeast Method*

This saffron-flavoured bread is eaten during the Swedish celebration of St. Lucias' day, December 13th. The festival is one that celebrates both Lucia, an early Christian martyr, and the beginning of the Christmas season. Young Swedish girls often dress up as "Lucia brides" adorned with crowns of candles and leaves and serve the Lucia bread to family and friends for breakfast.

| | |
|---|---|
| 2 pkgs | *active dry yeast* |
| 1/2 cup | *warm water* |
| Pinch | *saffron\** |
| 1/2 cup | *lukewarm milk* |
| 1/2 cup | *sugar* |
| 1 tsp. | *salt* |
| 2 | *eggs, beaten* |
| 1/4 cup | *margarine, softened* |
| 4 1/2 - 5 cups | *all purpose flour* |
| 1/2 cup | *citron, chopped* |
| 1/4 cup | *blanched almonds, chopped* |
| 1 Tbsp. | *lemon peel, grated* |
| | *Confectioners' Icing* |
| | *Green and red candied cherries* |

1) In a large bowl, sprinkle yeast over warm water; let stand until dissolved.
2) Stir saffron into milk. Add milk mixture, sugar, salt, eggs, butter and 2 1/2 cups of flour to the yeast mixture. Beat with an electric mixer until smooth.
3) Stir in citron, almonds, and peel with a wooden spoon. Add enough remaining flour to make a soft dough.
4) Turn dough out onto a lightly-floured surface. Knead about 10 minutes until smooth and elastic.
5) Place dough into a greased bowl, turning once to coat all over. Cover and let rise in a warm, draft-free place about 1 1/2 hours until double in bulk.
6) Punch dough down; with a sharp knife cut off 1/3 of dough and reserve for top braid. Cut remaining dough into 3 equal portions. Roll each portion into a rope about 24 inches long. Place ropes close together on a greased baking sheet. Braid ropes together starting from the centre and working to one end (as for Kolach). Turn the pan and braid the other end. When braided shape dough into a circle and pinch ends together to seal.

7) Divide reserved piece of dough into 3 equal portions; roll each into a 16-inch rope. Braid as above on a separate greased baking sheet.

8) Cover both braided rings. Let rise in a warm, draft-free place for about 45 minutes until double in bulk, but not long enough for braids to lose their definition.

9) Bake at 375° F for 20 - 25 minutes. Remove from the oven and cool completely on wire racks.

10) When loaves are cool, make 6 holes in the top of the small wreath for the candles. Drizzle Confectioners' Icing over both braids and decorate with cherries. Place small braid on top of large braid, insert candles in top braid before serving.

\* Substitute 2 - 3 drops of yellow food colouring if you don't have saffron.

**Icing:** Beat together 1 cup icing sugar and 1 Tbsp water, adding more water if icing is too thick to drizzle.

Makes one.

**Chappatis**

Indian breads are made from many different grain flours ranging from whole wheat to rice, and all are made without yeast. The most familiar of these are probably Chappatis, a Northern Indian bread made from whole wheat flour. Chappatis are served hot with a little "ghee" (clarified butter) or filled with curry, wrapped and eaten out of the hand.

| | |
|---|---|
| 1 1/2 cups | whole wheat flour |
| 3/4 cup | all-purpose flour |
| 1/4 tsp | salt |
| 1 1/4 Tbsp | ghee or vegetable oil |
| 1 to 1 1/4 cups | water |

1) In a large bowl, combine whole wheat flour, all-purpose flour and salt. Add ghee and mix well.
2) Make a well in the centre of the mixture and add enough water to make a soft dough. All the dough should be gathered into a ball in the bowl.
3) Stretch and knead the dough in the bowl until it is smooth and the sides of the bowl are clean. The more kneading you do, the lighter the bread will be.
4) Cover and let the dough rest for 30 - 40 minutes at room temperature in a draft-free place.
5) Turn dough out onto a lightly-floured surface. With a sharp knife, divide the dough into 10 - 12 equal pieces and form each into a ball.
6) Roll out each ball into a 6-inch circle about 1/8 inch thick. Make sure they are uniformly thick so they cook properly. Keep uncooked chappatis covered so they don't dry out.
7) Preheat oven to 450° F. Place 2 ungreased baking sheets in the oven while it preheats, to warm them. When the oven is hot, remove the sheets and arrange the breads on them. Return the sheets to the oven and bake the bread

for 2 minutes until they are firm to the touch. Increase the heat to broil and cook the chappatis for 2 more minutes or until they are puffed up and hollow at the centre. Watch carefully so they do not burn. Serve immediately.
Makes 10-12.

**Moroccan Bread**

## Traditional Yeast Method

Morocco is a warm country on the Northern tip of Africa. It is known for its many seasonings and spices — aniseed, cinnamon, peppercorns, cumin and coriander. The breads of the country reflect this heritage. This loaf is likely to be prepared in the home and then carefully carried to the communal bakery where it is baked along with many other loaves in huge clay or stone ovens.

| | |
|---|---|
| 1 pkg. | active dry yeast |
| 1 tsp. | sugar |
| 2 cups | lukewarm water |
| 1 cup | whole wheat flour |
| 1/4 cup | olive oil |
| 1 Tbsp. | aniseed |
| 1 1/2 tsps | salt |
| 2 tsps | sesame seeds |
| 4 cups | all-purpose flour |
| | Cornmeal |

1) In a small bowl, combine sugar and water, stir to dissolve sugar. Sprinkle yeast over the top and let stand for 10 minutes.
2) In a large bowl, combine whole wheat flour, oil, aniseed, salt and sesame seeds. Stir yeast mixture and add to dry ingredients.

3) Blend mixture, then beat with electric mixer until smooth. Add 2 cups of all-purpose flour, 1/2 cup at a time, beating after each addition.

4) Gradually add enough remaining flour, stirring with a wooden spoon, to make a stiff dough.

5) Turn dough out onto a lightly-floured surface and knead until smooth and elastic, about 10 minutes.

6) Return dough to a clean, greased bowl, turning once to coat the top. Cover and let rise in a warm, draft-free place about 1 1/2 hours or until double in bulk.

8) Punch dough down and with a sharp knife divide it in half. Form each half into a ball and let these rest 5 - 10 minutes.

9) On a lightly-floured surface, roll out each half into a round about 3/4 inch thick. Place on separate baking sheets that have been sprinkled with cornmeal.

10) Cover and let rise 45 - 60 minutes or until double in bulk. Prick rounds with a fork in several places around the outside edges.

11) Bake at 400° F for 10 minutes, reduce heat to 325° F and continue baking for 25 minutes or until loaves are golden and sound hollow when rapped.

12) Cool completely on wire racks.

Makes two loaves.

## Canadian Bannock

Bannock originated in Scotland and Northern England and was brought to Canada by the early fur traders and settlers. It soon became a staple of the native and pioneer diets, as they adapted what ingredients and baking methods were available at the time. Bannock is delicious baked in the oven or over the campfire and spread with butter and jam.

| | |
|---|---|
| 2 3/4 cups | all purpose flour |
| 2 tsps | baking powder |
| 1/2 tsp. | salt |
| 3 Tbsps | lard |
| 2/3 cup | water |

1) Preheat oven to 425° F.
2) In a bowl, combine flour, baking powder and salt; stir well.
3) With a pastry blender or 2 knives, cut in the lard until the mixture resembles coarse crumbs.
4) Gradually stir in water with a fork until dough is soft and slightly sticky.
5) Turn dough out onto a lightly-floured surface and knead gently 8-10 times until smooth.
6) Roll or pat dough into a circle 1/2 inch thick.
7) Bake on a greased baking sheet for 12 - 15 minutes or until golden brown. Alternatively, place dough in a cast iron frypan on top of the stove or on the hot ashes of the campfire (turn bannock over to brown both sides).
8) Cut into wedges and serve hot.

Makes one.

## Fried Bread Rounds

*Quick bread method*

These delicious fried rounds are an example of original Canadian baking at its best. The native peoples, using ingredients introduced by white newcomers, first used this recipe. It is very similar to bannock, only it is deep fried instead of baked. These rounds can be served hot as a meal accompaniment, or spread with butter and honey to eat anytime.

| | |
|---|---|
| *2 cups* | *all-purpose flour* |
| *1 1/2 tsps* | *baking powder* |
| *1/2 tsp.* | *salt* |
| *1/8 tsp.* | *baking soda* |
| *1 1/4 cup* | *buttermilk* |
| | *Vegetable oil* |

1) In a large bowl, combine flour, baking powder, salt and soda. Stir until well blended.
2) Gradually pour in buttermilk, stirring constantly. Add enough buttermilk to make a soft but not sticky dough.
3) Turn dough out onto a lightly-floured surface. Knead several times (about 30 seconds) until dough is smooth.
4) Roll dough out to a 1/2-inch thickness, cut into 3-inch rounds.
5) Heat oil (at least 1 - 1 1/2 inches deep) in a deep skillet over medium heat. Cook rounds a few at a time, until puffed and golden brown, about 4 - 5 minutes per side. Remove from oil and drain well on paper towels. Serve warm.

Makes 10-12.

# *Troubleshooting*

### Your dough didn't rise:

- water used to dissolve yeast was either too cool so yeast couldn't work or too hot, killing the yeast
- the place where the dough was set to rise was too cool
- the dough wasn't beaten vigorously enough and gluten formation was inhibited
- too much flour was added creating too stiff a dough

### Your bread didn't rise in the oven:

- yeast used was too old
- the place where dough was set to rise was too warm
- the dough was left too long, rising in the pans, before baking

### Baked bread is sticky inside and has a coarse texture:

- you have under-baked the loaf
- your oven temperature was incorrect (oven temperatures vary, check yours with a good oven thermometer)
- dough did not rise long enough before baking

## Baked bread is heavy and compact:

- too much flour was used, creating too stiff a dough
- some flours, such as whole wheat or rye, produce heavier products than those made with all-white flour
- the dough did not rise long enough before baking

## The bread crumbles:

- dough was left to rise too long before baking. This causes over-fermentation of the yeast and can result in a strong yeasty smell. Conditions in your kitchen greatly affect the rising of the dough — use the double in bulk test to check rising dough
- dough was not mixed well enough
- the place where dough was rising was too warm
- oven temperature was too low

## Bread has a large air space beneath crust:

- bread was over-baked
- dough was not covered while it was rising and crusted over
- dough did not rise long enough before baking
- not enough shortening or fat was used in preparation

## Bread has air bubbles or holes in it:

- all gas bubbles were not removed from dough when shaping the loaves. Press bubbles out by hand or firmly with rolling pin while shaping

## Loaves are too small:

- too large a pan size was used for the amount of dough
- dough did not rise long enough before baking

# Loaves are too large and poorly shaped:

- pans used were too small for amount of dough
- too much yeast was added
- dough was left too long rising in the pans before baking

# Bread has a large break or slash on its side:

- oven temperature was too hot
- loaves were improperly shaped
- dough did not rise long enough before baking

# Bread did not brown evenly:

- pans were too shiny and reflected heat away from the baking bread
- too many pans were in the oven so heat did not circulate evenly around them

# Breads' top crust cracked:

- the dough was left uncovered during final rising and crusted over
- the baked loaf was cooled too quickly by a cold draft
- the dough was left to rise in a cool draft

# OTHER HOMEWORLD TITLES

### ATTRACTING BIRDS

ISBN 0-919433-87-1     64 pp.     5 1/2 x 8 1/2     $6.95

### NORTHERN BALCONY GARDENING

ISBN 0-919433-98-7     64 pp.     5 1/2 x 8 1/2     $6.95

### JAMS AND JELLIES

ISBN 0-919433-90-1     48 pp.     5 1/2 x 8 1/2     $4.95

### PICKLES AND PRESERVES

ISBN 0-919433-88-X     48 pp.     5 1/2 x 8 1/2     $4.95

### HERBS FOR NORTHERN GARDENERS

ISBN 0-919433-99-5     64 pp.     5 1/2 x 8 1/2     $6.95

### LIVING ON YOUR OWN

ISBN 1-55105-018-8     64 pp.     5 1/2 x 8 1/2     $6.95

### CHRISTMAS SURVIVAL GUIDE

ISBN 1-55105-019-6     64 pp.     5 1/2 x 8 1/2     $6.95

### FURNITURE REFINISHING MADE EASY

ISBN 1-55105-022-6     64 pp.     5 1/2 x 8 1/2     $6.95

---

Look for these and other Lone Pine books at your local bookstore. If they're unavailable, order direct from:

Lone Pine Publishing
#206 10426-81 Avenue
Edmonton, Alberta   T6E 1X5
Phone: (403) 433-9333    Fax: (403) 433-9646